MATH ON THE JOB

Keeping People Healthy

This could be you!

Rick Wunderlich

Crabtree Publishing Company
www.crabtreebooks.com

Crabtree Publishing Company
www.crabtreebooks.com

Dedicated by Rick Wunderlich
To my daughter Sarah, a registered nurse and a wonderful caregiver.

Author: Rick Wunderlich

Editorial director: Kathy Middleton

Editors: Reagan Miller, Janine Deschenes, and Crystal Sikkens

Photo research: Margaret Amy Salter

Designer: Margaret Amy Salter

Proofreader: Kathy Middleton

Production coordinator and prepress technician: Margaret Amy Salter

Print coordinator: Katherine Berti

Math Consultant: Diane Dakers

Special thanks to Christa Heeg

Photographs:
Shutterstock: © ChameleonsEye: p5 (top)

All other images by Shutterstock

Library and Archives Canada Cataloguing in Publication

Wunderlich, Rick, author
    Math on the job : keeping people healthy / Richard Wunderlich.

(Math on the job)
Includes index.
Issued in print and electronic formats.
ISBN 978-0-7787-2359-2 (bound).--
ISBN 978-0-7787-2365-3 (paperback).--
ISBN 978-1-4271-1740-3 (html)

    1. Medicine--Mathematics--Juvenile literature. 2. Mathematics--Juvenile literature. I. Title. II. Title: Keeping people healthy.

R853.M3W86 2016   j510.2'461   C2015-908042-8
                                             C2015-908043-6

Library of Congress Cataloging-in-Publication Data

Names: Wunderlich, Richard, author.
Title: Math on the job. Keeping people healthy / Richard Wunderlich.
Other titles: Keeping people healthy
Description: New York, New York : Crabtree Publishing Company, [2016] | Series: Math on the job | Includes index.
Identifiers: LCCN 2016002525 (print) | LCCN 2016004776 (ebook) | ISBN 9780778723592 (reinforced library binding : alk. paper) | ISBN 9780778723653 (pbk. : alk. paper) | ISBN 9781427117403 (electronic HTML)
Subjects: LCSH: Medicine--Juvenile literature. | Physicians--Juvenile literature. | Mathematics--Juvenile literature.
Classification: LCC RA776 .W96 2016 (print) | LCC RA776 (ebook) | DDC 610--dc23
LC record available at http://lccn.loc.gov/2016002525

Crabtree Publishing Company
www.crabtreebooks.com   1-800-387-7650

Printed in Canada/022016/IH20151223

Published in Canada
Crabtree Publishing
616 Welland Ave.
St. Catharines, ON
L2M 5V6

Published in the United States
Crabtree Publishing
PMB 59051
350 Fifth Avenue, 59th Floor
New York, New York 10118

Published in the United Kingdom
Crabtree Publishing
Maritime House
Basin Road North, Hove
BN41 1WR

Published in Australia
Crabtree Publishing
3 Charles Street
Coburg North
VIC 3058

Contents

Please note:
The standard and metric systems are used
interchangeably throughout this book.

Health Care Workers

People working in health care have important jobs! These are the people we turn to when we are hurt or sick. They use their knowledge and skills to help us feel better. Careers in health care can be both challenging and rewarding. Learning about new medicine, equipment, and technology make these careers especially challenging.

Health care professionals must not only be knowledgeable, but also kind and compassionate.

CAREER 1

MEDICAL DOCTOR

Doctors are extremely well educated. They study math and science. They must have a university education with very high grades. Getting into medical school is very competitive. Only students with top marks and a lot of volunteer experience are accepted to medical schools.

Doctors complete at least four years of university, followed by four years of medical school. After medical school, doctors continue their training under the supervision of experienced doctors.

Think Like a Medical Doctor

Imagine you are a doctor working in the emergency room of a major hospital. A young boy is brought into the "ER," or "emergency room." The boy has a sore on his leg. It is red and the boy is in pain. What would you do?

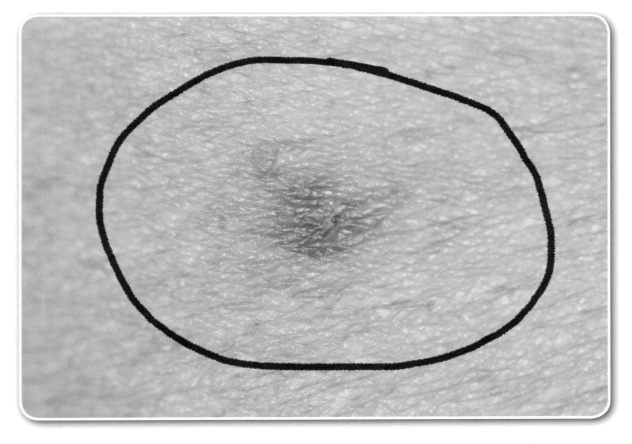

You examine the sore. It looks like an insect bite, so you ask the boy's father where they have been lately. He tells you they have been hiking and camping in a forest for a week. You suspect that the boy has been bitten by a spider and the bite has become **infected**. You **prescribe** an **antibiotic**, which is a kind of medicine that fights infections. You then use a marker to draw a circle around the spider bite on the boy's leg.

You tell the boy's parents to bring him back to the E.R. if the red area around the bite spreads and touches the circle.

SOLVE:

1. You prescribe medication to help ease the boy's pain. You prescribe a total of 15 tablets. The boy is to take half of one tablet every four hours. How many hours of pain relief will 15 tablets provide?

2. You also prescribe an antibiotic for the infection. The antibiotic is in liquid form. Each dose is 5 milliliters (ml). There are 1,000 ml in a liter (L). How many doses are there in ¼ liter container?

3. If a 5 ml dose is to be given every 6 hours, how long will a ¼ liter of liquid antibiotic last?

A few days later, the boy's father brings his son back to the ER to see you. He tells you that the boy's infection seems to be getting worse. You examine the boy and find he has a fever. You look at the sore, and although the red part hasn't spread to reach the circle you drew earlier, the boy tells you he is in a lot of pain.

ANALYZE:

You are concerned that the infection might be spreading throughout the boy's body. You decide to keep him in the hospital.

1 You give the boy more antibiotics through an intravenous drip, or **IV.** You give him 250 milliliters of antibiotics, which will drip from a bag over time. If the bag was empty after 5 hours, how many milliliters per hour was given to the boy?

2 At the same time, the boy is also given fluids through an IV to make sure his body has the liquids it needs. The IV is set to give the boy a 1-liter bag of fluid over 5 hours. How much IV fluid is given to the boy every hour?

3 You decide to give the boy something to reduce the **inflammation**. The amount of medicine you should give at each dose depends on the boy's weight. The dose is 0.125 milligrams (mg) per 1 kilogram (kg). If the boy weighs 40 kg, how many milligrams of medicine should be given in one dose?

TOUGH DECISION:

You continue to check on the boy every day. After a few days, you see that the redness has started to spread past the circle you drew around the sore. This means the infection is spreading.

1 You look at the boy's **chart** and see that the boy's temperature was 99.1 degrees Fahrenheit at noon, 99.5°F at 1 p.m., and 99.9°F at 2 p.m. Is the boy's temperature changing at a steady rate? How do you know?

2 It is now 5 p.m. You take the boy's temperature and find it is 101.1°F.

a) Since 98.6°F is the normal body temperature, how much above normal is the boy's temperature?

b) How many degrees did the boy's temperature rise since noon?

c) Would you continue giving the boy the same antibiotics, or would you try giving him a stronger antibiotic? Why?

1 You examine the boy's leg and see it is getting worse. If the infection grows too much, the boy's leg could be permanently damaged. The shape of the red area has grown to become a rectangle 10 cm long and 8 cm wide. What is the **approximate** area, in square cm, of the infection? (Tip: Area = length x width)

2 You decide to talk to the boy's parents and suggest that the boy see a **surgeon** about having an operation to treat the infected leg. Review the boy's temperature changes. How might you show the temperature **data** to the parents in a visual way that helps explain your concern for the boy's health?

The boy's parents agree that he should see a surgeon. It is the right decision! After surgery, the boy's fever has gone away and the infection has cleared up.

10 cm

8 cm

MATH TOOLBOX

GRAPHING

One way to show how the boy's temperature changed over time is to use a line graph. A line graph usually shows time on the horizontal axis and temperature on the vertical axis. Below is an example of a line graph. Using this example, create your own line graph using the boy's temperature data.

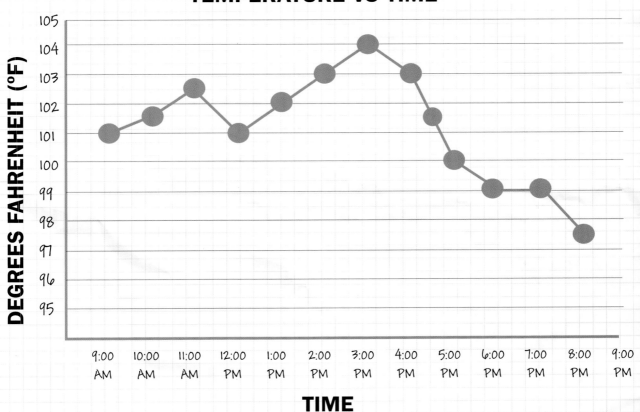

TEMPERATURE VS TIME

DEGREES FAHRENHEIT (°F)

TIME

WANT TO BE A MEDICAL DOCTOR?

1. Stay in school! A great education with a focus on math and science is a great beginning. College courses such as anatomy, biology, and chemistry can help.

2. Visit your school guidance counselor or local library and ask about universities that have medical schools.

3. Take a first aid course through the Red Cross and experience medical training.

CAREER

PATHWAYS

This could be you!

CAREER 2

REGISTERED NURSE

A registered nurse (RN) is part of a health care team devoted to the care and well-being of a wide variety of patients. Registered nurses must know about recording data, maintaining charts, taking blood, giving medications, and checking bandages. Registered nurses must also know how to use technology. Different departments in hospitals are often organized into floors, or wards. For example, nurses on duty in the maternity ward will help deliver babies. Nurses on surgical wards will assist during operations and care for patients as they recover. There are many different jobs in hospitals for nurses.

Nurses can specialize in a number of fascinating areas, from public health to surgery. Some nurses take extra training where they learn to care for patients directly, without a doctor supervising their work. They are called nurse practitioners.

Think Like a Registered Nurse

Imagine you are a registered nurse. You visit a new patient on your ward who is experiencing kidney problems. The kidneys control fluids in the body. The doctor's orders ask you to record the **volume** of liquid the patient drinks, and the volume of liquid given to the patients through their IV.

You are asked to record their **vital signs** every 45 minutes. There are four main vital signs. All are recorded in numbers. The four vital signs are:

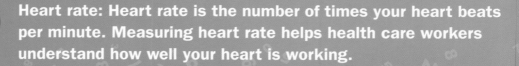

Body temperature: A normal body temperature is about 37°C or 98.6°F. A fever is a rise in body temperature. It is usually a sign of infection.

Blood pressure: Blood pressure measures the force of blood pushing against the sides of the blood vessels of the body. Measuring blood pressure shows how hard your heart has to pump to move blood through your body.

Heart rate: Heart rate is the number of times your heart beats per minute. Measuring heart rate helps health care workers understand how well your heart is working.

Breathing rate: Breathing rate is the number of breaths a person takes per minute. Knowing someone's breathing rate tells the nurse how well the patient is able to take in oxygen from the air.

Vital signs are important. These measurements are taken to help doctors and nurses understand a person's general health. They can also give clues to possible illnesses.

Each patient in a hospital has a chart with information about the patient's condition. Nurses measure vital signs and record the information on the patient's chart.

1 You know that there are 1,000 milliliters (ml) in a liter (L). The patient has drunk ¼ L of milk and 750 ml of water so far. How much fluid has the patient consumed in total? If the amount of fluid needed for this patient is 2 liters, how much more fluid do they need to consume that day?

2 Normal breathing **rates** for adults **range** between 12 and 18 breaths every minute. If the patient's breathing rate was 5 breaths every 10 seconds, how many breaths would that be in a minute? How much above the highest normal rate is that?

3 The patient is asking you for some pain reliever. The maximum amount of pain reliever is 3 grams per day, and the pain reliever comes in 300 milligram (mg) tablets.

a) What is the number of whole tablets you can give the patient in a day? There are 1,000 mg in a gram.

b) You look at the patient's chart and see that the patient has already received 2 ½ grams of pain reliever in the past 18 hours. You could also split a tablet in ½ or ¼ size pieces. How many more whole tablets and tablet **fractions** can you give the patient, without going over the maximum?

FACTS:

If your blood pressure is too high, the pressure can lead to a heart attack or stroke. If blood pressure is too low, it can indicate that something is wrong.

There are two different pressures measured for blood. One is called systolic pressure, which is the pressure in the tubes, called arteries, when the heart is pushing the blood out. The other is diastolic pressure, which is the pressure in the arteries when the heart is relaxed and filling with blood. A typical blood pressure is 120/80 (systolic/diastolic). The heart relaxes after pushing out blood, which is why the diastolic number is lower.

For adults, high blood pressure can be 140/90 or higher. Low blood pressure is 90/60 or lower.

TIME	TEMPERATURE
7:30 a.m.	37 °C
8:15 a.m.	37.4 °C
9:00 a.m.	37.8 °C
9:45 a.m.	38.2 °C
10:30 a.m.	38.6 •C
11:15 a.m.	_____

1 If your patients' blood pressure measured 160/110, would you say that they had high, normal, or low blood pressure?

2 Using the data from the table to the left, you make a line graph that shows the person's temperature versus the time their temperature was taken. Use your line graph to predict the next temperature reading.

3 The patient takes 4 breaths in 15 seconds. How many breaths is that in 1 minute? Explain your calculations.

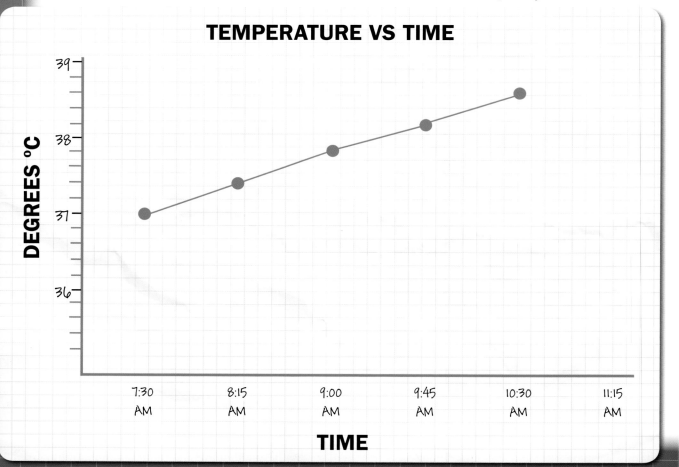

TEMPERATURE VS TIME

TOUGH DECISION:

One of the major tasks of a registered nurse is to listen to patients and try to answer their questions. Imagine you were in a patient's room and he said to you "Will you explain to me the difference between a heart rate of 80 and a blood pressure of 120/80? I don't understand what the numbers mean."

1 Nurses are extremely busy. If your schedule meant you had to move on to the next patient, how would you try to respond to the patient's question?

2 If you only had time to explain the answer in the quickest way possible, what would you say?

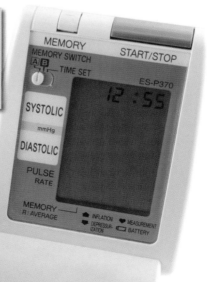

This is a portable machine that measures blood pressure. Registered nurses might use this machine in hospitals.

ROUNDING

Rounding numbers can help make sense of numbers with a lot of digits. To round a number to one decimal place, look at the digit in the second decimal place. If it is 5 or more, make that digit zero and round the digit in the first decimal place up by one. If the second digit is 4 or less, make the second digit zero and the first number stays as it is.

To convert 23 inches to feet you divide 23 by 12, since there are 12 inches in 1 foot.

23 / 12 = 1.916666667

That many digits are not needed. You need to estimate **using rounding.**

Rounding involves deleting unneeded numbers. In the example to the left, you are trying to find the number of feet in 23 inches. Rounding to one decimal place would make the number easier to understand. The answer would be 1.9, because the digit in the second decimal place, 1, is less than 5.

NAME: Christa Heeg
POSITION: Registered Nurse

How do you use math in your career?

While I was in nursing school, we had to pass a math test every semester in order to be allowed to do our clinical placements [training at medical sites]. I now use division and multiplication every day when I draw up patients' medications. For example, if I have to give a patient 0.5 mg of medicine and the medicine comes in a 5 mg container, I have to calculate the right dose from the container. Some medications are also given by a person's weight, so we use math to figure out the right amount to give. Sometimes patients need blood, which comes in bags of different sizes. A doctor tells me how many hours to give the blood for, and I calculate how many ml of blood should be given each hour. I also have to make simple conversions between units of measurement, such as ml to L.

This could be you!

WANT TO BE A REGISTERED NURSE?

1. Stay in school! A great education with a focus on science and math is the key. Many colleges and technical schools require that students take particular courses before they can be admitted to a nursing program. For example, you might have to take senior math classes in high school.

2. Visit your school guidance counselor or local library and ask about colleges and technical schools that offer registered nursing programs.

3. Explore whether there are hospital volunteer programs in your area. You get to help in the hospital, assist patients, and learn about what working in a hospital is like.

CAREER PATHWAYS

NUTRITIONIST

A nutritionist is a health care professional who advises people on how food affects their health. They assist patients by examining their current diets and making recommendations for changes that would improve their health.

Think Like a Nutritionist

Suppose you are asked to visit a patient in a hospital who has just been diagnosed with Crohn's disease. Crohn's is a condition that affects the **intestines**. People with Crohn's disease can be sensitive to certain kinds of foods. This causes digestion problems and stomach pain.

Before you visit the patient, you look at his medical records. You find the patient's weight has dropped from 142 pounds to 113 pounds in 3 months. His height is 5 feet 6 inches. The patient has started taking a new medicine for Crohn's disease, but it won't begin to help for several months. Your job is to create a healthy diet plan that will help the patient return to his normal weight. The diet plan must also avoid any foods that the patient is sensitive to.

1 How many pounds has the patient lost?

2 Over how many weeks did the patient lose the weight?

3 Calculate how much weight the patient lost per week. Round the answer to one decimal place.

The table below helps nutritionists find the healthy body mass index (BMI) range for men and women of various heights. Body mass index (BMI) is a measure of body fat based on a person's weight in relation to his or her height. BMI is most commonly used for adults over the age of 20.

1 You determine that a healthy weight gain goal for your patient is 2 pounds per week. Approximately how long would it take for the patient to reach his original weight of 142 pounds?

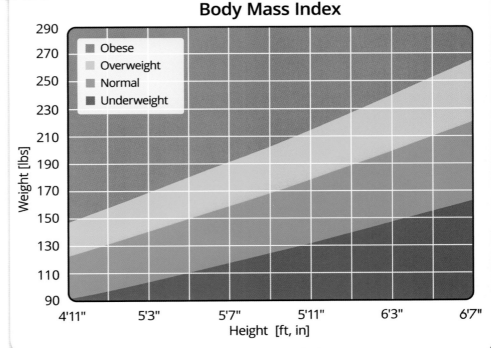

Body Mass Index

Calculating BMI

Metric:
With the metric system, the formula for BMI is weight in kilograms divided by height in meters squared (kg/m2). (Since height is commonly measured in centimeters, divide height by 100 to get height in meters.) To convert it to meters squared, multiply your answer by itself.

Standard:
When using pounds and inches, the formula needs to be altered slightly. Multiply weight in pounds by 703. Divide that by your height in inches squared. (To convert your height to inches squared, multiply your height by itself. For example, if you are 50 inches tall, you would multiply 50 x 50 to get your height in inches squared.)

You visit the patient and explain that foods that are hard to digest can often cause pain for people with Crohn's disease. You ask him if he has noticed if particular foods bother him. He responds that foods such as raw apples, corn, and blueberries often cause pain and cramps.

1 Suppose you advise the patient to stay away from these raw foods and try eating a ¼ cup serving of cooked fruit, such as applesauce, each day instead. If 10 medium apples make 1 quart of applesauce, how many days will 1 quart last the patient? There are 4 cups in a quart.

2 Suppose your patient says they like to eat applesauce as long as it's sweetened. You prefer the patient avoids sugar and artificial sweeteners. Before you advise the patient on what they should do, you do the calculations below to find out how much sugar and calories are in the applesauce.

a) The 1-quart applesauce recipe calls for ¼ cup of brown sugar and a ½ cup of white sugar. How much sugar is that all together?

b) If a cup of each type of sugar has 760 calories, and an apple has 53 calories, how many calories are in the recipe?

c) Calculate the number of calories in a ¼ cup serving. (Remember: 1 quart = 4 cups)

CONVERSION FACTOR

To increase the number of servings in a recipe, divide the number of servings you want by the number of servings in the recipe to find a conversion factor. This is the number that will make up the difference in recipe size. Multiply each item in the recipe by the conversion factor to find the correct amount of ingredients to use.

For example, if a recipe makes 4 servings, and you want to make 6 servings,

6 divided by 4 = 1.5.

1.5 is the **conversion** factor. If the recipe calls for 2 cups of flour,

2 x 1.5 = 3.

The new amount for the 6-serving recipe is 3 cups of flour.

WANT TO BE A NUTRITIONIST?

1. Stay in school! A great education with a focus on science and math is the key. Begin by getting a university degree in nutritional sciences.

2. Nutritionists are experts in healthy eating. Keep track of the foods you eat each day and then use the information in this book and other sources to find ways to include more healthy foods in your diet.

CAREER PATHWAYS

This could be you!

Learning More

Websites

This link gives examples to show how doctors, nurses, and other healthcare professionals use math:

http://mathcentral.uregina.ca/beyond/articles/medicine/med1.html

In this video, a nutritionist discusses her work including how she helps people eat healthy foods, and teaches families how to keep track of what they're eating:

www.bls.gov/k12/content/students/videos/video.htm

This link from the Kids' Health website focuses on nurses. Information includes the different places they work, jobs performed, and required skills and education:

http://kidshealth.org/kid/feel_better/people/nurses.html#

Books

Bell, Samantha. *Sports Medicine Doctor*. 21st Century Skills Library: Cool STEAM Careers. Cherry Lake Publishing, 2015.

Glasscock, Sarah. *How Nurses Use Math*. Chelsea House, 2010.

Minden, Cecilia. *Lunch By The Numbers*. Real-World Math: Cherry Lake Publishing, 2008

ANSWERS

Career 1: Medical Doctor

Solve: 1. 15 tablets × 2 = 30 half tablets; 30 × 4 hours = 120 hours, or 5 days

2. 1000 ml ÷ 5 ml = 200 doses per liter; 200 ÷ 4 = 50 doses in ¼ liter

3. 50 doses × 6 hours = 300 hours ÷ 24 hours = 12 ½ days

Analyze: 1. 250 ml ÷ 5 hours = 50 ml of antibiotics was given every hour.

2. 1 liter = 1000 ml; 1000 ml ÷ 5 = 200 ml every hour

3. 40 kg x 0.125 mg = 5 mg. One dose contains 5 mg.

Tough Decision: 1. Yes, it's rising 0.4 degrees every hour.

2. a) 101.1° - 98.6° = 2.5°. The temperature is 2.5° above normal.

b) 101.1° - 99.1° = 2.0°. The boy's temperature rose 2° since noon.

c) Give him a stronger antibiotic. The one he is on doesn't seem to be working since the infection is spreading.

Glossary

anatomy The science of the bodily structures of animals, including humans and plants

antibiotic A medicine that kills bacteria

approximate Close but not exact

biology The science of life, in all of its forms

chart In hospitals, a medical record that documents everything about a patient, from their entry into the hospital until they leave

chemistry The science of matter and substances

conversion To change a number to an equivalent amount

data Factual information in numbers, used for reasoning or calculations

estimate To judge the amount of something approximately

fraction A value given by one number divided by another

infected Containing disease caused by bacteria, viruses, or parasites

inflammation Describing symptoms such as redness, swelling, pain, and heat in an area of the body

intestine The lower end of the digestive canal

intravenous (IV) Giving medicine into the veins of a patient

prescribe To give a written direction to give medicine to a patient

range The difference between the highest and lowest values in a list of numbers

rate A ratio of two numbers that are related to each other. Miles per hour is a rate.

surgeon A medical doctor who performs surgeries, or operations

vital signs Measurements of heart rate, blood pressure, temperature, and breathing rate

volume A measurement of the amount of space a substance takes up

ward In hospitals, divided areas for different departments

ANSWERS CONTINUED

Career 1: Medical Doctor
Decide: 1. The infected area is 10 × 8 = 80 sq cm.
    2. Show the boy's parents a graph, which shows the rise in his temperature.

Career 2: Registered Nurse
Solve: 1. 1000 ml ÷ 4 = 250 ml; 250 + 750 = 1000 ml, or 1 liter. Fluids consumed so far is 1 liter, so 1 more liter is needed to reach a total of 2 liters.

Math Toolbox:

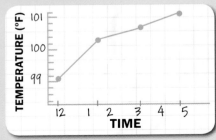

Index

Author Bio:

Rick Wunderlich greatly admires the medical workers who provide such wonderful care to those who are sick or injured. Rick has written math and science textbooks and has had the best job in the world for him, a teacher. He also gets queasy watching medical procedures.

ANSWERS CONTINUED
Career 2: Registered Nurse

Solve: 2. 60 seconds in a minute ÷ 10 seconds = 6; 6 × 5 breaths = 30 breaths per minute. 30 - 18 = 12. The patient's breathing rate is 12 breaths above the highest range for normal breaths per minute.

3. a) 3 g × 1000mg = 3000 mg; 3000 ÷ 300 = 10 tablets/day
b) 3 g per day - 2 ½ g = ½ g ; ½ g × 1000 mg = 2500 mg. Give 1 whole tablet (300 mg) plus a ½ tablet (150 mg) which leaves 50 mg without going over the 3000/day limit.

Analyze: 1. That blood pressure is in the "high" category.

2. The table shows a pattern of a temperature increase of 0.4 every 45 minutes. The next temperature is predicted to be 39 degrees.

3. 60 seconds in a minute ÷ 15 seconds = 4; 4 × 4 breaths = 16 breaths in 1 minute.

Tough Decision: 1. Answers may vary.

2. The numbers are related, but 80 is a measure of the number of heart beats per minute, and 120/80 is a measure of pressure when the heart is pumping blood and when the heart is relaxed.

Career 3: Nutritionist

Solve: 1. The patient has lost 142 - 113 = 29 pounds.
2. Loss happened over 3 months × 4 weeks = 12 weeks
3. Weight lost per week is 29 ÷ 12 = 2.41, or 2.4 pounds

Analyze: 1. At 2 pounds per week, it would take approximately 29 ÷ 2 = 14 ½ weeks to lose the weight.

Solve: 1. 1 quart = 4 cups; 4 cups × 4 servings in one cup = 16 servings. At 1 serving a day, 1 quart would last 16 days.

2. a) ½ = ²⁄₄; ²⁄₄ + ¼ = ¾ cups of sugar all together
b) ¾ cup = 0.75; 0.75 x 760 = 570 calories in ¾ cup of sugar; 53 calories x 10 apples = 530; 570 + 530 = 1100 total calories in the recipe.
c) 1100 calories ÷ 4 = 275 calories per cup; 275 ÷ 4 = 68.75 calories per ¼ cup serving.